# The Little Ships

## The Heroic Rescue at Dunkirk in World War II

by LOUISE BORDEN

illustrated by
MICHAEL FOREMAN

SCHOLASTIC INC.

For Harry Elliott and for all those
whose courage made the "miracle" possible
—L.B.

To all who sailed in the little ships
—M.F.

"Through the long time the story will be told;
Long centuries of praise on English lips,
Of courage godlike and of hearts of gold
Off Dunkerque beaches in the little ships."

*John Masefield, Poet Laureate, 1940*

"O God, be good to me.
Thy sea is so wide
And my ship is so small."

*Fisherman's Prayer*

ISBN 978-1-338-26428-9

Text copyright © 1997 by Louise Borden. Illustrations copyright © 1997 by Michael Foreman. All rights reserved. Published by Scholastic Inc., 557 Broadway, New York, NY 10012, by arrangement with Margaret K. McElderry Books, an imprint of Simon & Schuster Children's Publishing Division. SCHOLASTIC and associated logos are trademarks and/or registered trademarks of Scholastic Inc.

The publisher does not have any control over and does not assume any responsibility for author or third-party websites or their content.

12 11 10 9 8 7 6 5 4 3 2                    17 18 19 20 21 22

Printed in the U.S.A.                          40

First Scholastic printing, November 2017

Designed by Ann Bobco
The text of this book was set in Weiss.
The illustrations were rendered in watercolor.

## Foreword

In the summer of 1940 I had the honor to command His Majesty's Motor Torpedo Boat (MTB) 102. I was a lieutenant in the Royal Navy, aged twenty-one. In late May and early June of that year, the disaster and miracle of Dunkirk occurred. MTB 102 was part of it, making some seven trips from Dover in southeast England to Dunkirk, forty-five miles away in France. During the evacuation, MTB 102 was used largely as a despatch vessel. On the last night she carried the Admiral Afloat and controlled bringing off the French rearguard. She was the third-last warship to leave Dunkirk on June 4th.

Every five years, the Association of Dunkirk Little Ships (the surviving remnants of the intrepid band of assorted boats and yachts that contributed so much to the miracle of Dunkirk) makes a pilgrimage back to Dunkirk. MTB 102 has taken part in this in 1980, 1985, 1990, and 1995, and I have been invited to go in her, with the special honor of bringing "my ship" into harbor.

In 1995 I was surprised and delighted to find that we had Louise Borden with us, making the trip to get the authentic feeling of what it was like, for the benefit of the moving story she has written about the Dunkirk Escape. While details of her story are invented, it could have happened, and things like it actually did happen. It is a story very much in the spirit of that memorable summer of 1940.

Christopher Dreyer

In 1940,
I lived with my father in the town of Deal, on the Kent coast of England,
safe from the thunder
of the Germans' guns in France.
Some days in May I could hear it,
rolling in big booms across the English Channel.
Some days I could feel it,
rattling the glass in the windows on our street.

My father, Martin Gates, owned the *Lucy*,
a sturdy fishing smack.
Her wooden tubs were thick and heavy
and smelled of herring
and mackerel
and cod.
I liked to watch my father's quick hands,
stacking tubs and sorting fish.
I liked to listen to Dad's friends
trading stories on the beach.
They were all Deal fishermen too.

But now their talk was about
the trouble at Dunkirk,
just across the Channel,
only fifty miles away.
British soldiers were trapped there, they said.
Thousands and thousands.
And so were the French.
The Germans and their tanks would capture them.
Families would lose all those men who were
uncles and brothers
and fathers and sons.
Every boat on the English coast
was needed to go and help.
The owners
were to report for orders,
and for maps, and charts.

My brother, John, was a British soldier,
fighting in France.
Maybe he was in this trouble too.
Maybe he was trapped on the beaches of Dunkirk
and was waiting for a navy ship,
or a fishing boat like the *Lucy*,
to bring him home.

Fishermen on the beach
said I was my father's daughter.

I could set an anchor
and coil a rope
and nudge speed into the *Lucy*'s old engine
better than some of the village men
who were signing up to go to Dunkirk.
Like Mr. Lewis, who worked at the post office,
Mr. Cribben, the locksmith,
and Mr. Marsh, who had taught geometry to John.

So I pulled on a wool cap of my father's
that smelled of herring,
and a patched pair of John's outgrown trousers.
Only my father knew it
was me.

"Hurry! . . . Not much time! . . .
Too many men. . . . Not enough ships!"
Those were the words we heard echoing in town
and up and down the beach.
I hurried to help Dad
stack cans of water.
I lugged more cans, full of fuel, and yards of rope.
And I hurried again
to haul the wet nets off the *Lucy*.
"We'll need every inch of room for soldiers,"
my father called to me over his shoulder.
"Maybe even John,"
I called back.

That afternoon we sailed for Dunkirk.
Dad didn't have much time for talk.
He kept his words in his hands,
stowing a rope ladder
and checking the engine gears.
And he kept his words in his eyes,
reading the Channel charts and maps,
scanning the sky, thick with clouds.
My father wasn't famous,
but he knew about the sea and the tides and currents
and how to steer clear of the Goodwin Sands.
He was the one who had taught me to read a compass.
And he could name all the stars at night
like the explorers I had studied in school.

So on the last day of May the *Lucy* left Deal
and sailed north to Ramsgate
to join a motley group of ships.
All kinds were in her convoy.
Farther out in the Channel,
past the Goodwins,
our group joined with others.
It was like an amazing armada.
*Armada.*
It was a word from my schoolbook.
And there I was,
in the middle of the biggest armada of all.

That day
the line of convoys going to help rescue the British Army
was almost five miles long,
stretched end to end
on a smooth gray sea.
To save time and fuel,
tugboats and bigger ships
pulled little ships in their wakes.
A lot of towropes frayed and snapped.
A lot of rusty motors sputtered and stopped.

I listened to the low throb
of the *Lucy*'s engine.
Hour after hour.
Mile after mile.
Steady engine.
Steady friend.

The dozens of ships around us
were headed to Dunkirk too.
The littlest ships looked even smaller
under that sullen Channel sky.

Everyone in the boats around the *Lucy*
knew there was terrible trouble up ahead.

Big navy ships passed with their white wakes,
going the other way.
Headed back from Dunkirk,
to England and to home.
They made a silent parade.
Not grand.
Just uniform brown
and battleship gray.
Their decks and railings were crowded with men.
I tried to look up and find John
in that sea of tin helmets and tired faces.
But they were the faces of strangers
and not my tall skinny brother.

Dad handed me a mug
of strong, sweet tea,
and a woolly thick jacket
to keep off the Channel chill.
When our convoy reached the French coast,
we heard the German guns.
Other guns were answering back.

And then the *Lucy* was there,
off Dunkirk's beaches,
in the night
and in the early morning,
and it was real.
All the oily smoke that got in my eyes,
and all the terrible noise that got in my ears.
And all the men.
The sandy beaches at Dunkirk were black
with lines that curved like snakes.
And the lines were British soldiers.
And the French were there too.
There were even men standing shoulder to shoulder
along the length of the Mole,
the narrow wooden pier in Dunkirk's harbor.
Thousands of soldiers, waiting for ships.

We stayed close to a minesweeper,
then sailed into the shallows
to ferry our first load.
I called back the depth of the water
as Dad steered the *Lucy* toward the beach.
Not a beach like Deal's.
This beach was wide and flat,
its sand covered by men who were hungry and thirsty,
by horses running loose from their French riders,
by dozens of barking dogs,
by trucks and equipment,
by the wild mess of an army on the run.

And there were hundreds of other ships
that were little like ours—
English and French, Belgian and Dutch.
We were all there rowing
and carrying
and paddling
and ferrying—
from the sand beaches to the big ships
anchored out in deeper water
and back again.

My father gazed at the thousands of men
and I knew that he was thinking about John.

He stood at the helm,
holding the *Lucy* steady in the water,
against the wakes from other ships,
against broken planks washing toward the beach,
against lost boots and army coats,
and everything that soldiers leave behind
when they can take only themselves.

I kept checking the *Lucy's* fuel.
When only two cans were still full,
we followed a Smoky Joe*
and a Dutch skoot**
and turned to head home.
My father and I prayed that John, if he were here,
had found a place on a sturdy ship.
Suddenly the sky was filled with the noise of an enemy plane.
It was a dive-bombing German Stuka.
Some stray bullets hit the *Lucy*
and she sprang a dozen leaks.
Our last load of soldiers
had to bail with their helmets
on the miles going home.
But the *Lucy's* engine kept running steady
with that throb I knew so well.

* A *Smoky Joe* was a nickname used in the British Navy for a minesweeper.
** A *skoot* is a flat-bottomed Dutch boat, originally known as a *schuit*.

And then we were there,
with dozens of other ships,
streaming into the safety of the harbor at Dover.
Bringing our army home . . .

I helped my father look for John
among all the ships
unloading men.
I asked busy officers
who were yelling orders,
but no one could tell me news.
The ships crowding the harbor
were full of tall skinny soldiers.
But none were John Gates from Deal.

Mr. Lewis and Mr. Marsh spotted the *Lucy*,
and came to tell us how they'd been towed
by a Scottish trawler,
all the way back to the white cliffs of Dover.
And then they looked away, and said Mr. Cribben
wouldn't ever be coming home.

And so we went back to Deal,
and sailed the *Lucy* onto the narrow beach.
We kept the black, matted dog
that a French sergeant had asked us to take.
I named him Smoky Joe.

Smoky, with his damp rope collar,
was a part of Dunkirk
that we brought home to Deal.

On June 3,
we got word that John
had come back safely on a Belgian tug.
And the very next day,
I sat by the radio
with my father and Smoky Joe.

I sat straight up
when the Prime Minister thundered his grand speech.
I was glad that Mr. Churchill didn't keep
his words in his hands and in his eyes
in the way of Deal fishermen.
At first he had thought
only a few men could be saved
from the beaches of Dunkirk.
He was wrong.
The newspaper later said
over 338,000 men came home.
But I think Mr. Churchill knew all along
that our country could do it,
if everyone pulled together.
That's why he sent all those big navy ships.
And the little ships,
like our *Lucy*,
too.

# Author's Note

In May of 1940, many countries in Europe were at war with Germany. British and French soldiers, half a million of them, were trapped on three sides of northern France by German troops and tanks. The only way out for the Allied army, the only escape, was the sea.

An incredible armada of 861 ships, the largest at the time in naval history, assembled off the beaches of Dunkirk to ferry British and French soldiers across the English Channel to Dover and other small ports in southeastern England. Vice Admiral Bertram Ramsay, who organized these rescue efforts, directed "Operation Dynamo" from his headquarters in the chalk cliffs of Dover, just across the Channel from Dunkirk. He called the rescue armada his "Cockleshell Fleet" because of the hundreds of small river and coastal fishing craft that answered the government's call to assist the larger ships of the British Royal Navy.

Of the 338,226 men rescued, most came back to England on the bigger ships. But the little ships had their part to play during the crucial nine days, May 26–June 4, ferrying hungry and exhausted soldiers from Dunkirk's beaches across the dangerous shallow water to the bigger ships. Many dogs that were pets of English and French soldiers, and a few strays, were rescued as well. Almost two hundred dogs were aboard ships landing in Dover. There are as many stories about Dunkirk as there were ships and people involved. This story is part truth, part fiction. It could have happened. Maybe, indeed, it did.

## From Winston Churchill's June 4 speech to Parliament:

"We must be very careful not to assign to this deliverance the attributes of a victory. Wars are not won by evacuations. . . .

Even though large tracts of Europe and many old and famous States have fallen or may fall into the grip of the Gestapo and all the odious apparatus of Nazi rule, we shall not flag or fail. We shall go on to the end, we shall fight in France, we shall fight in the seas and oceans, we shall fight with growing confidence and growing strength in the air, we shall defend our island, whatever the cost may be, we shall fight on the beaches, we shall fight on the landing-grounds, we shall fight in the fields and in the streets, we shall fight in the hills; we shall never surrender, and even if, which I do not for a moment believe, this island or a large part of it were subjugated and starving, then our Empire beyond the seas, armed and guarded by the British Fleet, would carry on the struggle, until in God's good time, the New World, with all its power and might, steps forth to the rescue and liberation of the Old."